This Unicorn Gratitude Journal

BELONGS TO:

_____

DEDICATION

This Gratitude Journal For Kids is dedicated to all the Unicorn lovers out there who are full of ideas and want to share their grateful thoughts with the world (or NOT) and have fun in the process.

You are my inspiration for producing books and I'm honored to be a part of keeping all of your thoughts and ideas organized all in one easy to find spot.

How to use this Gratitude Journal:

This ultimate Gratitude notebook is a perfect way to track and record all your gratitude writing activities. This unique Gratitude logbook is a great way to keep all of your important and private information all in one place.

Each interior page includes prompts and space to record the following:

1. Date - Write the date of your journal entry.

2. Today I am grateful For - Use the lines here to record thoughts and things you are happy about.

3. What was the best part of your day - Stay on task using the space below to draw or write out the best part of each day.

4. My level of happiness - Record and track with these emoji faces, checkmark from 1-5 which face represents your day.

If you are new to gratitude journaling or have been at it for a while, this cute unicorn gratitude journal is a must have! Can make a great useful gift for anyone who desires more gratitude in their life or just loves Unicorns!

Enjoy!

TODAY I AM GRATEFUL FOR.. DATE:--------------

WHAT WAS THE BEST PART ABOUT YOUR DAY?
DRAW OR WRITE ABOUT IT!

MY LEVEL OF HAPPINESS

TODY I AM GRATEFUL FOR..   DATE:--------------

WHAT WAS THE BEST PART ABOUT YOUR DAY ?
DRAW OR WRITE ABOUT IT !

MY LEVEL OF HAPPINESS

TODAY I AM GRATEFUL FOR..   DATE:-------------

WHAT WAS THE BEST PART ABOUT YOUR DAY ?
DRAW OR WRITE ABOUT IT !

MY LEVEL OF HAPPINESS

TODAY I AM GRATEFUL FOR..   DATE:--------------

WHAT WAS THE BEST PART ABOUT YOUR DAY?
DRAW OR WRITE ABOUT IT!

MY LEVEL OF HAPPINESS

TODAY I AM GRATEFUL FOR.. DATE:-------------

WHAT WAS THE BEST PART ABOUT YOUR DAY?
DRAW OR WRITE ABOUT IT!

MY LEVEL OF HAPPINESS

TODY I AM GRATEFUL FOR..   DATE:--------------

WHAT WAS THE BEST PART ABOUT YOUR DAY ?
DRAW OR WRITE ABOUT IT !

MY LEVEL OF HAPPINESS

TODAY I AM GRATEFUL FOR..   DATE:-------------

WHAT WAS THE BEST PART ABOUT YOUR DAY ?
DRAW OR WRITE ABOUT IT !

MY LEVEL OF HAPPINESS

TODAY I AM GRATEFUL FOR..   DATE:-------------

- --
- --
- --
- --
- --
- --

WHAT WAS THE BEST PART ABOUT YOUR DAY?
DRAW OR WRITE ABOUT IT!

MY LEVEL OF HAPPINESS

TODY I AM GRATEFUL FOR..   DATE:-------------

- -
- -
- -
- -
- -
- -

WHAT WAS THE BEST PART ABOUT YOUR DAY?
DRAW OR WRITE ABOUT IT!

MY LEVEL OF HAPPINESS

TODAY I AM GRATEFUL FOR..   DATE:-------------

_____
_____
_____
_____
_____
_____
_____

WHAT WAS THE BEST PART ABOUT YOUR DAY?
DRAW OR WRITE ABOUT IT!

MY LEVEL OF HAPPINESS

TODAY I AM GRATEFUL FOR..   DATE:-------------

WHAT WAS THE BEST PART ABOUT YOUR DAY?
DRAW OR WRITE ABOUT IT!

MY LEVEL OF HAPPINESS

TODAY I AM GRATEFUL FOR.. DATE:-------------

WHAT WAS THE BEST PART ABOUT YOUR DAY?
DRAW OR WRITE ABOUT IT!

MY LEVEL OF HAPPINESS

TODY I AM GRATEFUL FOR..   DATE:--------------

WHAT WAS THE BEST PART ABOUT YOUR DAY ?
DRAW OR WRITE ABOUT IT !

MY LEVEL OF HAPPINESS

TODAY I AM GRATEFUL FOR..   DATE:--------------

- _____
- _____
- _____
- _____
- _____
- _____

WHAT WAS THE BEST PART ABOUT YOUR DAY ?
DRAW OR WRITE ABOUT IT !

MY LEVEL OF HAPPINESS

TODY I AM GRATEFUL FOR.. DATE:------------

WHAT WAS THE BEST PART ABOUT YOUR DAY?
DRAW OR WRITE ABOUT IT!

MY LEVEL OF HAPPINESS

TODAY I AM GRATEFUL FOR..   DATE:-------------

- _____
- _____
- _____
- _____
- _____
- _____

WHAT WAS THE BEST PART ABOUT YOUR DAY?
DRAW OR WRITE ABOUT IT!

MY LEVEL OF HAPPINESS

TODAY I AM GRATEFUL FOR..   DATE:----------------

WHAT WAS THE BEST PART ABOUT YOUR DAY ?
DRAW OR WRITE ABOUT IT !

MY LEVEL OF HAPPINESS

TODY I AM GRATEFUL FOR..   DATE:--------------

- _____
- _____
- _____
- _____
- _____
- _____

WHAT WAS THE BEST PART ABOUT YOUR DAY?
DRAW OR WRITE ABOUT IT!

MY LEVEL OF HAPPINESS

TODY I AM GRATEFUL FOR..　　　　　DATE:-----------

WHAT WAS THE BEST PART ABOUT YOUR DAY?
DRAW OR WRITE ABOUT IT!

MY LEVEL OF HAPPINESS

TODAY I AM GRATEFUL FOR..   DATE:-------------

WHAT WAS THE BEST PART ABOUT YOUR DAY?
DRAW OR WRITE ABOUT IT!

MY LEVEL OF HAPPINESS

TODAY I AM GRATEFUL FOR..   DATE:---------------

WHAT WAS THE BEST PART ABOUT YOUR DAY ?
DRAW OR WRITE ABOUT IT !

MY LEVEL OF HAPPINESS

TODAY I AM GRATEFUL FOR.. DATE:--------------

WHAT WAS THE BEST PART ABOUT YOUR DAY?
DRAW OR WRITE ABOUT IT!

MY LEVEL OF HAPPINESS

TODAY I AM GRATEFUL FOR..   DATE:-------------

WHAT WAS THE BEST PART ABOUT YOUR DAY ?
DRAW OR WRITE ABOUT IT !

MY LEVEL OF HAPPINESS

TODAY I AM GRATEFUL FOR..   DATE:--------------

- ------------------------------------
- ------------------------------------
- ------------------------------------
- ------------------------------------
- ------------------------------------
- ------------------------------------

WHAT WAS THE BEST PART ABOUT YOUR DAY?
DRAW OR WRITE ABOUT IT!

MY LEVEL OF HAPPINESS

TODY I AM GRATEFUL FOR.. DATE:--------------

WHAT WAS THE BEST PART ABOUT YOUR DAY?
DRAW OR WRITE ABOUT IT!

MY LEVEL OF HAPPINESS

TODAY I AM GRATEFUL FOR.. DATE:---------------

- ------------------------------------
- ------------------------------------
- ------------------------------------
- ------------------------------------
- ------------------------------------
- ------------------------------------
- ------------------------------------
- ------------------------------------

WHAT WAS THE BEST PART ABOUT YOUR DAY ?
DRAW OR WRITE ABOUT IT !

MY LEVEL OF HAPPINESS

TODAY I AM GRATEFUL FOR..   DATE:-------------

WHAT WAS THE BEST PART ABOUT YOUR DAY?
DRAW OR WRITE ABOUT IT!

MY LEVEL OF HAPPINESS

TODAY I AM GRATEFUL FOR..   DATE:-------------

WHAT WAS THE BEST PART ABOUT YOUR DAY ?
DRAW OR WRITE ABOUT IT !

MY LEVEL OF HAPPINESS

TODY I AM GRATEFUL FOR..   DATE:--------------

WHAT WAS THE BEST PART ABOUT YOUR DAY ?
DRAW OR WRITE ABOUT IT !

MY LEVEL OF HAPPINESS

TODAY I AM GRATEFUL FOR..   DATE:--------------

- _____
- _____
- _____
- _____
- _____
- _____
- _____

WHAT WAS THE BEST PART ABOUT YOUR DAY ?
DRAW OR WRITE ABOUT IT !

MY LEVEL OF HAPPINESS

TODAY I AM GRATEFUL FOR..   DATE:------------

WHAT WAS THE BEST PART ABOUT YOUR DAY?
DRAW OR WRITE ABOUT IT!

MY LEVEL OF HAPPINESS

TODAY I AM GRATEFUL FOR..   DATE:-------------

_____
_____
_____
_____
_____
_____
_____

WHAT WAS THE BEST PART ABOUT YOUR DAY?
DRAW OR WRITE ABOUT IT!

MY LEVEL OF HAPPINESS

TODAY I AM GRATEFUL FOR..   DATE:-------------

WHAT WAS THE BEST PART ABOUT YOUR DAY?
DRAW OR WRITE ABOUT IT!

MY LEVEL OF HAPPINESS

TODY I AM GRATEFUL FOR..   DATE:--------------

- _____
- _____
- _____
- _____
- _____
- _____

WHAT WAS THE BEST PART ABOUT YOUR DAY?
DRAW OR WRITE ABOUT IT!

MY LEVEL OF HAPPINESS

TODAY I AM GRATEFUL FOR..   DATE:-------------

WHAT WAS THE BEST PART ABOUT YOUR DAY ?
DRAW OR WRITE ABOUT IT !

MY LEVEL OF HAPPINESS

TODAY I AM GRATEFUL FOR..   DATE:-------------

WHAT WAS THE BEST PART ABOUT YOUR DAY?
DRAW OR WRITE ABOUT IT!

MY LEVEL OF HAPPINESS

TODAY I AM GRATEFUL FOR..   DATE:------------

WHAT WAS THE BEST PART ABOUT YOUR DAY?
DRAW OR WRITE ABOUT IT!

MY LEVEL OF HAPPINESS

TODY I AM GRATEFUL FOR..   DATE:---------------

_____
_____
_____
_____
_____
_____

WHAT WAS THE BEST PART ABOUT YOUR DAY ?
DRAW OR WRITE ABOUT IT !

MY LEVEL OF HAPPINESS

TODAY I AM GRATEFUL FOR..   DATE:------------

WHAT WAS THE BEST PART ABOUT YOUR DAY ?
DRAW OR WRITE ABOUT IT !

MY LEVEL OF HAPPINESS

TODAY I AM GRATEFUL FOR..   DATE:--------------

WHAT WAS THE BEST PART ABOUT YOUR DAY ?
DRAW OR WRITE ABOUT IT !

MY LEVEL OF HAPPINESS

TODAY I AM GRATEFUL FOR..   DATE:---------------

WHAT WAS THE BEST PART ABOUT YOUR DAY ?
DRAW OR WRITE ABOUT IT !

MY LEVEL OF HAPPINESS

TODAY I AM GRATEFUL FOR..   DATE:--------------

_____
_____
_____
_____
_____
_____
_____
_____

WHAT WAS THE BEST PART ABOUT YOUR DAY?
DRAW OR WRITE ABOUT IT!

MY LEVEL OF HAPPINESS

TODAY I AM GRATEFUL FOR..   DATE:-----------

WHAT WAS THE BEST PART ABOUT YOUR DAY?
DRAW OR WRITE ABOUT IT!

MY LEVEL OF HAPPINESS

TODAY I AM GRATEFUL FOR..   DATE:---------------

- _____
- _____
- _____
- _____

WHAT WAS THE BEST PART ABOUT YOUR DAY ?
DRAW OR WRITE ABOUT IT !

MY LEVEL OF HAPPINESS

TODAY I AM GRATEFUL FOR..   DATE:--------------

WHAT WAS THE BEST PART ABOUT YOUR DAY?
DRAW OR WRITE ABOUT IT!

MY LEVEL OF HAPPINESS

TODAY I AM GRATEFUL FOR.. DATE:----------

WHAT WAS THE BEST PART ABOUT YOUR DAY?
DRAW OR WRITE ABOUT IT!

MY LEVEL OF HAPPINESS

TODAY I AM GRATEFUL FOR..   DATE:-------------

WHAT WAS THE BEST PART ABOUT YOUR DAY ?
DRAW OR WRITE ABOUT IT !

MY LEVEL OF HAPPINESS

TODAY I AM GRATEFUL FOR.. DATE:-------------

- --
- --
- --
- --
- --
- --

WHAT WAS THE BEST PART ABOUT YOUR DAY ?
DRAW OR WRITE ABOUT IT !

MY LEVEL OF HAPPINESS

TODAY I AM GRATEFUL FOR..   DATE:--------------

WHAT WAS THE BEST PART ABOUT YOUR DAY?
DRAW OR WRITE ABOUT IT!

MY LEVEL OF HAPPINESS

TODAY I AM GRATEFUL FOR..   DATE:---------------

WHAT WAS THE BEST PART ABOUT YOUR DAY?
DRAW OR WRITE ABOUT IT!

MY LEVEL OF HAPPINESS

TODAY I AM GRATEFUL FOR..   DATE:-------------

WHAT WAS THE BEST PART ABOUT YOUR DAY ?
DRAW OR WRITE ABOUT IT !

MY LEVEL OF HAPPINESS

TODAY I AM GRATEFUL FOR..   DATE:-------------

WHAT WAS THE BEST PART ABOUT YOUR DAY?
DRAW OR WRITE ABOUT IT!

MY LEVEL OF HAPPINESS

TODAY I AM GRATEFUL FOR..   DATE:---------------

WHAT WAS THE BEST PART ABOUT YOUR DAY ?
DRAW OR WRITE ABOUT IT !

MY LEVEL OF HAPPINESS

TODAY I AM GRATEFUL FOR..   DATE:-------------

WHAT WAS THE BEST PART ABOUT YOUR DAY ?
DRAW OR WRITE ABOUT IT !

MY LEVEL OF HAPPINESS

TODAY I AM GRATEFUL FOR.. DATE:-------------

WHAT WAS THE BEST PART ABOUT YOUR DAY ?
DRAW OR WRITE ABOUT IT !

MY LEVEL OF HAPPINESS

TODAY I AM GRATEFUL FOR..   DATE:-------------

- _____
- _____
- _____
- _____
- _____
- _____

WHAT WAS THE BEST PART ABOUT YOUR DAY ?
DRAW OR WRITE ABOUT IT !

MY LEVEL OF HAPPINESS

TODAY I AM GRATEFUL FOR..   DATE:-------------

WHAT WAS THE BEST PART ABOUT YOUR DAY?
DRAW OR WRITE ABOUT IT!

MY LEVEL OF HAPPINESS

TODAY I AM GRATEFUL FOR..   DATE:-------------

- _____
- _____
- _____
- _____
- _____
- _____
- _____

WHAT WAS THE BEST PART ABOUT YOUR DAY?
DRAW OR WRITE ABOUT IT!

MY LEVEL OF HAPPINESS

TODY I AM GRATEFUL FOR.. DATE:----------

WHAT WAS THE BEST PART ABOUT YOUR DAY?
DRAW OR WRITE ABOUT IT!

MY LEVEL OF HAPPINESS

TODAY I AM GRATEFUL FOR..   DATE:--------------

_____
_____
_____
_____
_____
_____

WHAT WAS THE BEST PART ABOUT YOUR DAY ?
DRAW OR WRITE ABOUT IT !

MY LEVEL OF HAPPINESS

TODY I AM GRATEFUL FOR..   DATE:--------------

WHAT WAS THE BEST PART ABOUT YOUR DAY ?
DRAW OR WRITE ABOUT IT !

MY LEVEL OF HAPPINESS

TODY I AM GRATEFUL FOR..   DATE:-------------

- _____
- _____
- _____
- _____

WHAT WAS THE BEST PART ABOUT YOUR DAY?
DRAW OR WRITE ABOUT IT!

MY LEVEL OF HAPPINESS

TODAY I AM GRATEFUL FOR.. DATE:------------

WHAT WAS THE BEST PART ABOUT YOUR DAY?
DRAW OR WRITE ABOUT IT!

MY LEVEL OF HAPPINESS

TODAY I AM GRATEFUL FOR.. DATE:---------------

- _____
- _____
- _____
- _____
- _____
- _____

WHAT WAS THE BEST PART ABOUT YOUR DAY ?
DRAW OR WRITE ABOUT IT !

MY LEVEL OF HAPPINESS

TODAY I AM GRATEFUL FOR..   DATE:-------------

WHAT WAS THE BEST PART ABOUT YOUR DAY ?
DRAW OR WRITE ABOUT IT !

MY LEVEL OF HAPPINESS

TODAY I AM GRATEFUL FOR..   DATE:-------------

- _____
- _____
- _____
- _____
- _____
- _____

WHAT WAS THE BEST PART ABOUT YOUR DAY?
DRAW OR WRITE ABOUT IT!

MY LEVEL OF HAPPINESS

TODAY I AM GRATEFUL FOR..   DATE:-------------

WHAT WAS THE BEST PART ABOUT YOUR DAY?
DRAW OR WRITE ABOUT IT!

MY LEVEL OF HAPPINESS

TODAY I AM GRATEFUL FOR..   DATE:-------------

WHAT WAS THE BEST PART ABOUT YOUR DAY ?
DRAW OR WRITE ABOUT IT !

MY LEVEL OF HAPPINESS

TODAY I AM GRATEFUL FOR..   DATE:----------

WHAT WAS THE BEST PART ABOUT YOUR DAY ?
DRAW OR WRITE ABOUT IT !

MY LEVEL OF HAPPINESS

TODAY I AM GRATEFUL FOR..   DATE:--------------

- _____
- _____
- _____
- _____
- _____

WHAT WAS THE BEST PART ABOUT YOUR DAY ?
DRAW OR WRITE ABOUT IT !

MY LEVEL OF HAPPINESS

TODAY I AM GRATEFUL FOR..   DATE:-------------

WHAT WAS THE BEST PART ABOUT YOUR DAY ?
DRAW OR WRITE ABOUT IT !

MY LEVEL OF HAPPINESS

TODAY I AM GRATEFUL FOR.. DATE:--------------

- --
- --
- --
- --
- --
- --
- --

WHAT WAS THE BEST PART ABOUT YOUR DAY?
DRAW OR WRITE ABOUT IT!

MY LEVEL OF HAPPINESS

TODAY I AM GRATEFUL FOR..   DATE:--------------

WHAT WAS THE BEST PART ABOUT YOUR DAY ?
DRAW OR WRITE ABOUT IT !

MY LEVEL OF HAPPINESS

TODAY I AM GRATEFUL FOR..   DATE:---------------

WHAT WAS THE BEST PART ABOUT YOUR DAY ?

DRAW OR WRITE ABOUT IT !

MY LEVEL OF HAPPINESS

TODY I AM GRATEFUL FOR.. DATE:-------------

WHAT WAS THE BEST PART ABOUT YOUR DAY ?
DRAW OR WRITE ABOUT IT !

MY LEVEL OF HAPPINESS

TODAY I AM GRATEFUL FOR..　　　　DATE:-------------

_____
_____
_____
_____
_____
_____
_____

WHAT WAS THE BEST PART ABOUT YOUR DAY?
DRAW OR WRITE ABOUT IT!

MY LEVEL OF HAPPINESS

TODY I AM GRATEFUL FOR..   DATE:----------------

WHAT WAS THE BEST PART ABOUT YOUR DAY?
DRAW OR WRITE ABOUT IT!

MY LEVEL OF HAPPINESS

TODAY I AM GRATEFUL FOR..　　　　　DATE:-------------

- _____
- _____
- _____
- _____
- _____
- _____

WHAT WAS THE BEST PART ABOUT YOUR DAY ?
DRAW OR WRITE ABOUT IT !

MY LEVEL OF HAPPINESS

TODAY I AM GRATEFUL FOR..   DATE:------------

WHAT WAS THE BEST PART ABOUT YOUR DAY ?
DRAW OR WRITE ABOUT IT !

MY LEVEL OF HAPPINESS

TODAY I AM GRATEFUL FOR..   DATE:-------------

- _____
- _____
- _____
- _____

WHAT WAS THE BEST PART ABOUT YOUR DAY?
DRAW OR WRITE ABOUT IT!

MY LEVEL OF HAPPINESS

TODAY I AM GRATEFUL FOR..   DATE:-------------

WHAT WAS THE BEST PART ABOUT YOUR DAY ?
DRAW OR WRITE ABOUT IT !

MY LEVEL OF HAPPINESS

TODAY I AM GRATEFUL FOR..   DATE:--------------

WHAT WAS THE BEST PART ABOUT YOUR DAY ?

DRAW OR WRITE ABOUT IT !

MY LEVEL OF HAPPINESS

TODAY I AM GRATEFUL FOR..   DATE:------------

WHAT WAS THE BEST PART ABOUT YOUR DAY ?
DRAW OR WRITE ABOUT IT !

MY LEVEL OF HAPPINESS

TODAY I AM GRATEFUL FOR..   DATE:-------------

- _____
- _____
- _____
- _____
- _____
- _____
- _____
- _____

WHAT WAS THE BEST PART ABOUT YOUR DAY?
DRAW OR WRITE ABOUT IT!

MY LEVEL OF HAPPINESS

TODY I AM GRATEFUL FOR.. DATE:--------------

WHAT WAS THE BEST PART ABOUT YOUR DAY?
DRAW OR WRITE ABOUT IT !

MY LEVEL OF HAPPINESS

TODAY I AM GRATEFUL FOR..   DATE:--------------

- _____
- _____
- _____
- _____
- _____
- _____

WHAT WAS THE BEST PART ABOUT YOUR DAY?
DRAW OR WRITE ABOUT IT!

MY LEVEL OF HAPPINESS

TODAY I AM GRATEFUL FOR.. DATE:------------

WHAT WAS THE BEST PART ABOUT YOUR DAY ?
DRAW OR WRITE ABOUT IT !

MY LEVEL OF HAPPINESS

TODAY I AM GRATEFUL FOR..   DATE:-------------

- _____
  _____
- _____
  _____
- _____
  _____
- _____
  _____

WHAT WAS THE BEST PART ABOUT YOUR DAY ?
DRAW OR WRITE ABOUT IT !

MY LEVEL OF HAPPINESS

TODAY I AM GRATEFUL FOR..   DATE:-------------

WHAT WAS THE BEST PART ABOUT YOUR DAY ?
DRAW OR WRITE ABOUT IT !

MY LEVEL OF HAPPINESS

TODAY I AM GRATEFUL FOR.. DATE:---------------

_____
_____
_____
_____
_____
_____

WHAT WAS THE BEST PART ABOUT YOUR DAY ?
DRAW OR WRITE ABOUT IT !

MY LEVEL OF HAPPINESS

TODAY I AM GRATEFUL FOR..   DATE:-----------

WHAT WAS THE BEST PART ABOUT YOUR DAY ?
DRAW OR WRITE ABOUT IT !

MY LEVEL OF HAPPINESS

TODAY I AM GRATEFUL FOR..   DATE:-------------

- _____
- _____
- _____
- _____
- _____
- _____

WHAT WAS THE BEST PART ABOUT YOUR DAY?
DRAW OR WRITE ABOUT IT!

MY LEVEL OF HAPPINESS

TODAY I AM GRATEFUL FOR..   DATE:---------------

WHAT WAS THE BEST PART ABOUT YOUR DAY ?
DRAW OR WRITE ABOUT IT !

MY LEVEL OF HAPPINESS

TODAY I AM GRATEFUL FOR.. DATE:--------------

WHAT WAS THE BEST PART ABOUT YOUR DAY ?
DRAW OR WRITE ABOUT IT !

MY LEVEL OF HAPPINESS

TODAY I AM GRATEFUL FOR..   DATE:-------------

WHAT WAS THE BEST PART ABOUT YOUR DAY ?
DRAW OR WRITE ABOUT IT !

MY LEVEL OF HAPPINESS

TODAY I AM GRATEFUL FOR..   DATE:---------------

WHAT WAS THE BEST PART ABOUT YOUR DAY ?
DRAW OR WRITE ABOUT IT !

MY LEVEL OF HAPPINESS

TODAY I AM GRATEFUL FOR..   DATE:--------------

WHAT WAS THE BEST PART ABOUT YOUR DAY ?
DRAW OR WRITE ABOUT IT !

MY LEVEL OF HAPPINESS

TODAY I AM GRATEFUL FOR..   DATE:---------------

WHAT WAS THE BEST PART ABOUT YOUR DAY?
DRAW OR WRITE ABOUT IT!

MY LEVEL OF HAPPINESS

TODAY I AM GRATEFUL FOR..   DATE:-------------

WHAT WAS THE BEST PART ABOUT YOUR DAY ?
DRAW OR WRITE ABOUT IT !

MY LEVEL OF HAPPINESS

TODAY I AM GRATEFUL FOR..   DATE:-------------

- -
- -
- -
- -
- -
- -
- -

WHAT WAS THE BEST PART ABOUT YOUR DAY ?
DRAW OR WRITE ABOUT IT !

MY LEVEL OF HAPPINESS

TODAY I AM GRATEFUL FOR..   DATE:---------------

WHAT WAS THE BEST PART ABOUT YOUR DAY ?
DRAW OR WRITE ABOUT IT !

MY LEVEL OF HAPPINESS

TODY I AM GRATEFUL FOR..   DATE:-------------

- _____
- _____
- _____
- _____
- _____
- _____
- _____

WHAT WAS THE BEST PART ABOUT YOUR DAY?
DRAW OR WRITE ABOUT IT!

MY LEVEL OF HAPPINESS

TODAY I AM GRATEFUL FOR..   DATE:------------

WHAT WAS THE BEST PART ABOUT YOUR DAY?
DRAW OR WRITE ABOUT IT!

MY LEVEL OF HAPPINESS

TODAY I AM GRATEFUL FOR..   DATE:--------------

- _____
- _____
- _____
- _____

WHAT WAS THE BEST PART ABOUT YOUR DAY?
DRAW OR WRITE ABOUT IT!

MY LEVEL OF HAPPINESS

TODAY I AM GRATEFUL FOR..   DATE:-------------

WHAT WAS THE BEST PART ABOUT YOUR DAY?
DRAW OR WRITE ABOUT IT!

MY LEVEL OF HAPPINESS

TODAY I AM GRATEFUL FOR..   DATE:---------------

WHAT WAS THE BEST PART ABOUT YOUR DAY ?
DRAW OR WRITE ABOUT IT !

MY LEVEL OF HAPPINESS

TODAY I AM GRATEFUL FOR.. DATE:--------------

WHAT WAS THE BEST PART ABOUT YOUR DAY?
DRAW OR WRITE ABOUT IT!

MY LEVEL OF HAPPINESS

Lightning Source UK Ltd.
Milton Keynes UK
UKHW030622010322
399388UK00008B/517